You can't know it all … you never will. You may worry that you'll never know enough to see you safely through this world. But there is wisdom enough to see you through this world and into the next, if you choose to reach out and grasp it. This book will introduce you to a greater Book and its Author, a guidebook to an eternity that can be yours, if only you …

... have FAITH!

# have
# FAITH!

Ian Davidson

The Clarinda Press

Published in 2014 by the Clarinda Press
Copyright © 2014 by Ian Davidson

10 9 8 7 6 5 4 3 2 1

A CIP catalogue record for this book is
available from the British Library

ISBN 978-0-9930795-0-4

Printed and bound in Great Britain by
CPI Group (UK) Ltd, Croydon,
CR0 4YY

Cover design by Dog Whistle Design

*To*
*those seeking God*

# *Contents*

# Preface

My prayer and plea is that all who pick up this book will read it from cover to cover. It is not a large volume. In fact, it is quite small. I have deliberately tried to write as clearly, correctly, coherently and concisely as possible, as directed by R. W. Jepson in his book *Teach Yourself to Express Yourself*. Writing is not easy and I am far from a natural at it. But I have always wanted to pen a book on the Christian faith – and now, here it is!

I am under no illusion as to the task the Lord's body is facing in winning people to Christ. Humanism is making inroads and its influence can be seen in the number of humanist weddings and funerals now taking place everywhere. Church membership is not what it was and church buildings are regularly closing down. All I can say is: People don't know what they're missing!

My thanks go to the small Church of Christ that meets in Wallacestone, Scotland for financing the whole project. The other congregations in the Slamannan District Churches of Christ also endorsed the printing of this book. It is sent out with their love and concern for all readers. Each church is small in number, but each of the members is big of heart. I have lived with them all my life and I love them all in the Lord.

My thanks also go to my long-term next-door neighbour, David Witherow, who has helped me every step of the way in the preparation of this book. Without his expertise on the technical side of things, this volume would never have been published. David also read the draft of each chapter and his advice was always welcome; the more so since, striving to be a good editor, he always sought to help me find the best way to express Christian faith and truth as I have come to understand it, without seeking to interpose his own ideas or interpretations. I'm also grateful to Sue Burton for her comments and corrections.

I wish to point out that the use of 'he' and 'him' in this book does not mean the exclusion of she and her. I adopt the old rule that 'the masculine will be taken to include the feminine wherever necessary'.

Some chapter and verse or verses are quoted from various books of the Bible. It is important to have a Bible handy to check each quote and to read it within its context. The Bible is a collection of individual books, each of which is divided into numbered chapters, with each chapter containing several numbered verses. Therefore you can locate a quote by checking the contents page at the front of the Bible to find the page number of the particular book, then using the numbers printed at the start of each chapter and verse you can locate the quote within that book. For example (James 4:13-17) means go to chapter 4 of the book called James and read verses 13 to 17 inclusive. Remember that there may be slight differences in wording if your translation of the Bible differs from the particular translation from which the quote is taken.

I have quoted many writers on the Bible and its truths. To keep the book simple, I have not always quoted sources for these; where I have, I have not given exact references. I apologise to anyone I have failed to acknowledge, and I am, of course, grateful to all those whose understanding has deepened and strengthened my own.

For further study I recommend: *Seeing the Big Picture: A Christian's Guide to the Old Testament* by Dr Alastair Ferrie and *The New Testament Documents: Are They Reliable?* by Prof. F. F. Bruce.

Comments and questions on the contents of this book are most welcome. Please contact the author at:

iansneddondavidson@gmail.com

and he will get back to you.

# 1  The universe – God's universe!

The universe is big – very big. Distances are so vast that they have to be measured in light-years. Light travels at 186,000 miles or 300,000 kilometres per second. So a light-year is roughly 6 trillion miles or 9.5 trillion kilometres. That equates to around 12 million round trips to the moon.

The nearest star to the earth, after the sun, is Alpha Centauri, which is 4.3 light-years away. Our sun is 93 million miles from earth and so the distance to Alpha Centauri is over 250,000 times greater than that to the sun. A spacecraft such as the Voyager probe that has just entered interstellar space would take more than 80,000 years to reach Alpha Centauri. But 4.3 light-years is nothing compared with the distances to Andromeda (2.5 million light-years) and quasars (often more than 10 billion light-years).

Astronomers also tell us that there are 100,000 million, million, million stars in the universe; with the naked eye we can see only about 6,000. The Milky Way galaxy has 100 billion stars. But our galaxy is only one of around 100 billion such galaxies known to exist. These figures are mind-boggling.

Our sun is so large that well over a million earths could be poured into it. But how does it compare in size with the star VY Canis Majoris, which is a supergiant in the constellation Canis Major? This star is almost 4000 light-years from earth and it is 1,540 times bigger than the sun and 30,000 times brighter. It is so big that over 11 billion of our suns could fit inside it. Its diameter has been calculated at 1.22 billion miles or 1.96 billion kilometres. Think of a passenger plane flying around it. Just one flight all the way round Canis Majoris would take almost 800 years.

Never underestimate the importance of our sun. Without it, there could be no life on earth. Yet, only half a billionth of the sun's energy hits the earth and, in just one second, the sun releases more energy than mankind has produced since the beginning of creation. This immense amount of energy is generated by nuclear reactions. Hydrogen atoms are continuously combining to produce atoms of a heavier gas – helium. Each time an atom of helium is formed energy including light and heat is released and this is what makes the sun 'shine'. The surface temperature of the sun is around 6000° Celsius and the central temperature may reach 15,000,000° Celsius.

The sun, of course, is at the centre of the solar system. Its planets are: Mercury, Venus, Earth, Mars, Jupiter, Saturn, Uranus and Neptune. (Pluto is now classified as a dwarf planet.) The innermost planet Mercury goes round the sun quickly and so has a year of only 87.97 earth days, while the outermost planet Neptune takes 165 earth *years* to complete its orbit. Man has always been fascinated by these other planets and continues to probe them. There have been almost fifty attempts to send space probes to Mars, many of them failures but some spectacularly successful. The photographs sent back reveal a rocky and dead world. The earth, by comparison, is teeming with life. It is unique in our solar system.

So how did the universe get here? Scientists today argue that the universe began with a 'Big Bang', a phrase, incidentally, coined by a scientist, Sir Fred Hoyle, who didn't believe in any such thing. Here's the story. About 13.8 billion years ago the universe was born in a cosmic fireball. It spontaneously sprang out of a void or, to put it another way, it simply appeared out of nothing. So the proposition is that everything came from nothing, including you.

Imagine you are sitting in your house one day and outside you hear a big bang. You rush outside, a neighbour is there too and you ask him: 'What made that almighty bang?' He says: 'Oh, nothing, it just happened'. Would you be happy with his reply? Surely a cause is needed for such a bang. Surely a cause is needed for the Big Bang that produced the universe. As the famous *kalam* cosmological argument puts it: 'Whatever begins to exist has a cause. The universe began to exist. Therefore, the universe has a cause'. Or, more simply, as a popular car sticker tells us: 'Big Bang Theory of the Universe: God Spoke and Bang! There It Was'.

Another big question is: How do we account for all the complexity within the universe? The universe is so complex that brilliant minds like Sir Isaac Newton and Albert Einstein are needed to explain it. Do you understand all their mathematical equations? Newton's *Principia Mathematica* is arguably the greatest scientific work ever produced. Newton saw no conflict between his scientific studies and his belief in God. On the contrary, as the result of his discovery of the law of gravitation he was moved to admire even more the Designer in whom he believed. The same goes for such famous scientists as Johannes Kepler, Sir Humphry Davy, Sir David

Brewster, Michael Faraday, Louis Pasteur, Gregor Mendel, Lord Kelvin, Joseph Lister, James Clerk Maxwell, and many, many more.

What about the fine-tuned facts of the universe? Gravity is just right; critical density is just right; energy levels are just right; the distances of the sun and moon are just right; and, among other things, the earth's size, atmosphere, rotational speed and land-water ratio are just right. Sceptics say: 'There only appears to be design'. The theist says: 'The evidence from the universe points to the fact of design. The universe has been expertly thought out and brought into being. If it had been left to chance then the chances are we would not be here'.

How did life originate in the universe? It is a big question. The odds against life arising spontaneously on earth are so enormous as to make it impossible. The scientists Hoyle and Chandra Wickramasinghe have pointed out that the odds against life igniting accidentally are $10^{40000}$ to one.

Wickramasinghe has gone on to say: 'For life to have been a chemical accident on earth is like looking for a particular grain of sand on all the beaches in all the planets of the universe – and finding it'. Another scientist has said: 'The probability of life originating by accident is comparable to the probability of the unabridged dictionary resulting from an explosion in a printing shop'. Yet people go on believing the impossible because the only viable alternative, supernatural creation, is rejected out of hand. But why discount intelligent design?

The late Professor Antony Flew was once described as the world's most notorious atheist. He was so popular a thinker that his 1950 essay 'Theology and Falsification' became the most widely reprinted philosophical publication in the latter half of the twentieth century. He also published over thirty books. But before he died he changed his mind. His commitment to 'follow the argument wherever it leads' led him to believe that a God stands behind the rationality of nature. The structure of the cell and DNA had a big part to play in his 'conversion'. He writes, 'I now believe there is a God ... I now think it [the evidence] does point to a creative Intelligence almost entirely because of the DNA investigations. What I think the DNA material has done is that it has shown, by the almost unbelievable complexity of the arrangements which are needed to produce life, that intelligence must have been involved in getting these extraordinarily diverse elements to work together'.

The living cell is so complex that it is likened to a factory or a computer or an information processing machine. It is made up of 100 thousand million atoms. In other words, there is nothing primitive about a living cell. 'More complicated than the city of New York,' says one expert. Yet, cells are so small that two hundred of them could be placed on the dot of this letter ' i ' and there could be as many as 37 trillion of them in one human body; some have even suggested a figure of up to 50 trillion. Who's counting?

DNA (deoxyribonucleic acid) is a study in itself. It is reckoned that the human genome is over 3.5 billion letters long and would fill a whole library. The actual length of the DNA tightly coiled in each cell amounts to roughly 6.5 feet or 2 metres in length. Therefore, if we could unravel all the DNA in a human body then it would reach to the sun and back almost 235 times (remember, the sun is 93 million miles from earth). No wonder Nancy Pearcey has been led to say: 'The most powerful evidence for design in my own view is the DNA code'.

The first verse of the Bible reads: 'In the beginning God created the heavens and the earth'. So what it reveals is that Someone spoke the physical universe into existence and that Someone is God. Henry M. Morris has written:

> Not only does the first verse of the Bible speak of the creation of space and matter, but it also notes the beginning of time. The universe is actually a continuum of space, matter and time, no one of which can have a meaningful existence without the other two. The term matter is understood to include energy and must function in both space and time.

So when it comes to the origin of the universe, there are only two options: no one created something out of nothing, or else someone created something out of nothing. As Norman Geisler and Frank Turek have written: 'Which view is more reasonable? Nothing created something? No. Even Julie Andrews knew the answer when she sang, "Nothing comes from nothing. Nothing ever could!" And if you can't believe that nothing caused something, then you don't have enough faith to be an atheist'.

# 2 The Bible

We look at the universe and we see everywhere evidence of a creator – a god. But we might ask, so what? What has a god of atoms and stars to do with us? Well, God who took the trouble to shape the universe also shaped us, and on that basis we might reasonably expect Him to take a special interest in humanity: for even atheists will concede that man has yet to find any organism in creation more complex than himself.

So there is a God, a God who is concerned about us and about whom we must be concerned. The chapters to come will form an introduction to what is known about this mutual concern: about God and His Son Jesus and His Spirit; about humanity, about sin and salvation, and about death and resurrection.

But in this chapter we will, we must first look at how all this has come to be known. Not through gazing at stars or smashing atoms, and certainly not by inspecting the lint that has gathered in our navels, but through that evidence which is a gift from God Himself in an act of revelation: in the writing of His holy book, the Bible. Here and here alone is to be discovered God's love for us and his intent for us; if we are to have faith and if that faith is to grow to ripeness, we must be guided by its words.

The Bible is a well-known book, but not a well-read book. Many a person has started to read it through, but never got past Leviticus, which is the third book in. There is much to the Bible; it is made up of 66 books in total. It lives up to its name because the Greek word *biblia*, from which our English word is derived, actually is in the plural form, 'books'. So the Bible is a library of books. Each one is unique, but bring them all together and there is one harmonious whole. This is quite an achievement given the fact that the Bible was written by writers who lived hundreds of miles and hundreds of years apart. Christians believe that its unity is a gift from God.

The Bible stands out from every other book and, therefore, everyone should stand up and take notice of it. It should be read and studied by all. Why? Because the Bible reveals the mind of God, the state of man, the way of salvation, the doom of the ungodly and the happiness of believers. To ignore the Bible is to ignore the voice of God. To reject the Bible is to reject the truth. To oppose the Bible is to side with the devil. We must realise that a great spiritual war is continuously being fought over the hearts and minds of men and women everywhere. Like it or not, you are involved in this war of all wars in which there is no neutrality. For each of us, the reality is that the war will either end in heaven or in hell. The last book of the Bible assures us that victory will go to the godly. In the Good Book you find out how you get from the sinning side to the winning side. That's why you should read it for all its worth.

Pick up a copy of the Bible and in the table of contents is a list of books – books familiar and unfamiliar. For example, the names Genesis, Psalms and Revelation will probably be known to most, but not the names Obadiah, Zephaniah and Titus. You also observe there is a major division in the Bible between what are called: *The Books of the Old Testament* and *The Books of the New Testament.* There are 39 books in the Old Testament and 27 in the New. (Easy to remember because 3 x 9 = 27.) That's a lot of reading!

Make no mistake about it, the Bible was written to be understood. Yes, there are some things within it hard to understand, but with the right attitude and approach its message can be believed and obeyed, leading to the salvation of the soul. This is the essential business of the Bible: *Salvation*. Salvation has everything to do with the forgiveness of sins. God had a plan to save the world and that plan was centred on His Son, Christ Jesus. It is important always to remember that, as Jesus said during His ministry: 'For I did not come to judge the world but to save it' ( John 12:47b).

But Jesus did not come immediately after the fall of man (Genesis 3). God's plan was not completed overnight. The plan was carefully worked out over thousands of years. In these thousands of years mankind has lived through three ages. First, there was the starlight age, then the moonlight age and, finally, the sunlight age. The sunlight, gospel or Christian age has now been around for nearly two thousand years. It is the greatest era of them all because it is the era of the special kingdom – the kingdom of Christ – over which He reigns from heaven. It is into this kingdom all must be born ( John 3:1-8). We do not enter the natural kingdom without birth and we do not enter the spiritual kingdom without spiritual rebirth.

Another name for the starlight age is the patriarchal age, so named because in this age the father of the family acted as prophet, priest and king. A lot happened during this age about which we can read in the books of Genesis and Job. It has been the longest age so far in the history of the world. It lasted from the creation to the giving of the Law by Moses (Exodus 20). Henry M. Morris has written: 'Divine laws were given to men and women long before Moses. Abraham was guided by such laws: "Abraham obeyed my voice, and kept my charge, my commandments, my statutes, and my laws" (Genesis 26:5). Exactly how these primeval laws were given, and in what form, we do not know, for they have not been preserved'. And so the Bible tells us: mankind has never been without guidance in this world as to what is right and what is wrong; what is good and what is evil; what is truth and what is falsehood. This was true from the beginning; it is true today.

The moonlight age is the Mosaic age or Jewish age. God decided to work out His plans and purposes through a nation, the Jews, who are descended from the patriarchs: Abraham, Isaac, Jacob, and their heirs. Someone once said: 'In ancient days it is revealed that when each nation had chosen gods for itself, the God of heaven chose for Himself a nation'. So the Jews are a chosen people. From them came the promised Messiah, the Saviour of the world. Jesus came as a Jew, lived as a Jew, and died as a Jew. But He did not die for His nation only, but for all the nations of the world. The gospel of Christ is for everyone. In other words, God never forgot the Gentiles. In working through the Jews, He worked towards the salvation of all. Remember the words to Abraham: '… through your offspring all the nations of the earth will be blessed, because you have obeyed me' (Genesis 22:18).

The Old Testament books were originally written in the Hebrew language (there are a few verses in Aramaic), which is proof positive they were written primarily for the Jews. They contain instructional books, historical books, prophetical books and poetical books. They cover a period of around fifteen hundred years. A lot happened to the Jewish people in that time. They had their ups and downs – mostly downs. Sadly, too often they did not live up to the commandments of God. Instead, they let Him down again and again. His prophets tried to keep them on the straight and narrow, but, more often than not, to no avail. The people would not listen. They would not do as they were told. So God frequently punished them and many perished at the hands of their enemies. Two tribes survived – Judah and Benjamin. Their capital was Jerusalem. They too had their struggles and survived only through the providence of God. God kept an especially close eye on Judah because it was from this tribe that the future Messiah would come (Genesis 49:8-12; Revelation 5:5). The long history of the Jews is recorded in the Bible as a warning for us (1 Corinthians 10:11). We repeat their mistakes at our peril.

The sunlight age is the age in which we live. It began when God established Christ's kingdom on earth. That kingdom commenced on the day of Pentecost (Acts 2) – a day when around three thousand Jews became followers of Christ in Jerusalem. In the New Testament, the book of Acts tells us how, from that day, Christian congregations were established throughout the Roman world and how, even to this day, sinners are saved. The epistles written by Paul, Peter, James, John, Jude, and the unnamed writer of Hebrews reveal what is required to keep the saints, those who have been saved, on the right path. The book of Revelation – a prophetic book – shows us how Christ's kingdom will triumph over all earthly kingdoms and how victory belongs to Jesus, the Lamb of God whose sacrifice secured that victory.

The gospel records were written by Matthew, Mark, Luke (the only Gentile to contribute to the New Testament) and John. Why four gospel records? Matthew reveals Jesus is the King of the Jews; Mark shows He is the Son of Man; Luke declares He is the Saviour of the world; and John asserts He is the Son of God. For example, we read in John's gospel: 'Jesus did many other miraculous signs in the presence of His disciples, which are not recorded in this book. But these are written that you may believe that Jesus is the Christ, the Son of God, and that by believing you may have life in His name' (John 20:30,31). So we can say that John witnessed the facts; he recorded them; we read them; we believe them; and through faith in Jesus we obtain life, eternal life. From then on it is a life of service to the Master. We do not live to please ourselves, we live to please Him. Without the Bible, we would have no way of knowing any of this. That's why the Bible is so important to fallen mankind.

As was said at the beginning of the chapter, the Bible is a revelation from God. Yes, the words are the words of men, but they were all written under the inspiration of the Holy Spirit so as to make them also the words of God. Paul wrote: 'All Scripture is God-breathed and is useful for teaching, rebuking, correcting and training in righteousness, so that the man of God may be thoroughly equipped for every good work' (2 Timothy 3:16,17). When God breathes into something, that something comes alive. '... the Lord God formed the man from the dust of the ground and breathed into his nostrils the breath of life, and the man became a living being' (Genesis 2:7). Peter once said this of prophecy: 'Above all, you must understand that no prophecy of Scripture came about by the prophet's own interpretation. For prophecy never had its origin in the will of man, but men spoke from God as they were carried along by the Holy Spirit' (2 Peter 1:20,21). The writer of Hebrews put it this way: 'For the word of God is living and active. Sharper than any double-edged sword, it penetrates even to dividing soul and spirit, joints and marrow; it judges the thoughts and attitudes of the heart' (Hebrews 4:12). Given the above passages, we can safely say the Bible is unique. There is no other book like it. Through the ages authors come and authors go, but the Bible's Author goes on for ever.

The Bible has to be interpreted. Revelation is what God has said. Interpretation is what we think God meant by what He said. The former is perfect; the latter may not be. Nothing should be read out of context. And it helps to know the background of every book. In other words, who is writing to whom and when and where and why.

There are tremendous tools available today to all serious students of the Bible – translations, atlases, commentaries, dictionaries, concordances, handbooks, lexicons: all the apparatus of scholarship. Many wise men have spent a lifetime compiling books that can help us in our understanding of the Scriptures. Critics say it has all been a waste of time. But has it? We must all realise that what is at stake is eternal life and joy through eternity. Those who have laboured to help others achieve this goal through a better understanding of Scripture can hardly be said to have been wasting their time.

But please take note that no man-made book is perfect. Some books are even written to distort God's words. There are those who weave words to deceive the unwary. So be on your guard! It is good to read a good book on the Bible, but it is better to read and study the Bible itself. Methodical reading of the Scriptures will lead to a mindset tuned to God. An unvarying diet of television, tabloids and advertising will lead to a mindset tuned to trivia. Satan must be laughing up his diabolical sleeve at human folly. But Satan has the very opposite of concern for human salvation. For those of us who have accepted that our lives must be spent searching for and receiving this salvation offered by God, it's far from a laughing matter.

To understand the Bible requires attention to its language. Now language is either literal or figurative. It is a mistake to read literal language as figurative and figurative language as literal. The Bible, like many other books, contains both types. In it, there are examples of simile, metaphor, allegory, personification, irony, and other figures of speech. On reading the Bible, we soon realise, for example, that white stands for purity; light for goodness; darkness for evil; fire for judgment; a horse for war; a lion for strength; an eagle for swiftness and exaltation; a horn for power and the number seven for perfection. C. S. Lewis once pointed out that the Book of Revelation is full of wonderful imagery. There are symbols all over it. He concluded his remarks by saying: 'People who take these symbols literally might as well think that when Christ told us to be like doves, He meant that we were to lay eggs'.

The Bible tells us what is good and bad in the world. You can learn much by going through the Good Book and highlighting by different colours what God promotes and what God opposes. For example, God loves goodness, kindness, virtue, chastity, honesty, truthfulness, sincerity, discipline, love, peace, mercy, humility, generosity, patience, holiness, among others. He opposes hatred, lust, selfishness, faithlessness, deceit, adultery, pride, drunkenness, greed, vengeance, murder, hypocrisy, corruption, and the like. You will find that God is for all things good and Satan is for all things evil. The struggle between good and evil has been there from virtually the very beginning of the world. And so the war continues and the casualties mount. But, as we shall see later, God has done everything to save us and help us win through.

Another way to study the Bible is by topics, events or characters. Word studies can also be an eye-opener. Take, for example, the word 'testament' which we have already come across. What is involved in God's testaments? Why did God have to establish a new testament in His Son? What was the purpose of the old one and why was it taken out of the way? The Bible gives us the answers. Many Jews today are still trying to live by the Old Testament, which has animal sacrifice at the heart of it. Jews today do not offer sacrifices only because the temple and priest-hood needed for sacrifice are gone. But the New Testament tells all who read it that Jesus was the sacrifice to end all sacrifices. He offered Himself as a sacrifice for the sins of the whole world. He shed His life-blood on the cross of Calvary that all might be reconciled to God and be justified, sanctified and saved in His sight. The story of Jesus is the greatest story ever told. But one of the greatest tragedies in the history of the world is that so many of His people (the Jews) do not recognise Him for what He was and is: their long-awaited Messiah. Jesus fulfilled the Law or the Old Testament and took it out of the way. Those who are still trying to live by it are, sadly, living BC lives in an AD world.

The revelation of God is complete. As has been said: 'The Bible is perfect for its purpose and its purpose is to make us perfect or lacking in nothing'. Part of the introduction in a Gideon's Bible reads:

Its teaching is holy, its precepts are binding, its histories are true, its prophecies are certain and its decisions immutable. Read it to be wise, believe it to be safe, and practise it to be holy. It contains light to direct you, armour to protect you, food to sustain you, and comfort to cheer you ... Christ is its subject, our good its design, redemption its plan, and the glory of God its end. It is given to you here in this life, it will be opened in the judgment, and is established forever. It involves the highest responsibility, will reward the greatest labour, and condemns all who trifle with its sacred contents. Come to it with awe; read it with reverence, frequently, slowly, prayerfully.

Never write off the Bible because of its age. The Bible is not old, but right up to date. John Young put it well:

How can a book which is about men whose means of transport were limited to horses and camels (or feet) over land, and wind in sails or oars across the sea, have anything relevant to say to men who get to the moon? The trouble with this attitude is that it concentrates on surface differences. If we concentrate on clothes, or customs, or travel, we shall see ourselves as totally different from the men and women we read about in the Bible and conclude that the Bible cannot do anything useful today. But, in fact, similarities between the Bible characters and ourselves are enormous. The problems they faced were basically our problems – cost of living, war and peace, getting on with other people, and so on. We find in the Bible people who fell in love, people who hated, people who were anxious and afraid, people who worked, people who laughed and cried, people who fell ill, people who grew old, people who died. The Bible is about men and women like that, and activities like that. It deals with the 'constants' in human life and deals with them in a profound way. It was a book for the first century. It is a book for the twenty-first century. It is a book for all ages.

Remember! The Bible contains the wisdom which will lead the sinner to Jesus and so to God's forgiveness. But we must read it with care, with persistence, and with hunger for God's truth.

# 3  God

The God whom we meet in the pages of the Bible is the God who is omniscient, which is to say all-knowing, omnipotent, that is all-powerful, and omnipresent, present everywhere. The Bible never sets out to prove the existence of God. It assumes His existence. He was there from the beginning and indeed created that beginning and everything that followed. In his book *Who Made God?* the scientist Edgar Andrews writes:

> … we can see that Genesis 1:1 is making three distinct claims. Firstly, it asserts that there existed 'in the beginning' an entity (God) who of necessity stood outside the universe and was prior to it. Secondly, this God is further characterised as being capable of creating the universe *ex nihilo* – out of nothing. Thirdly, we are told that He did in fact create the universe in just this manner.

So the Bible is telling us, in so many words, that the

universe was caused by an uncaused prior cause and that uncaused prior cause is God.

The question of God's existence is the most important question a person can ask. Philosopher William Lane Craig in his book *On Guard* writes:

Now when I use the word *God* … I mean an all-powerful, perfectly good Creator of the world who offers us eternal life … If such a God does not exist, then life is absurd. That is to say, life has no ultimate meaning, value or purpose … If God does not exist, then both man and the universe are inevitably doomed to death. Man, like all biological organisms, must die. With no hope of immortality, man's life leads only to the grave. His life is but a spark in the infinite blackness, a spark that appears, flickers and dies.

John Blanchard in his outstanding book *Does God Believe in Atheists?* makes a telling observation:

Several years ago, *Encyclopaedia Britannica* published a set of fifty-four volumes which marshalled the writings of many eminent thinkers in the Western world on the most important ideas that have been studied and investigated over the centuries. The subjects covered included law, science, philosophy, history and theology; the longest essay of all was on the subject of God. Addressing the question as to why this should be the case, co-editor Mortimer Adler wrote: 'More consequences for thought and action follow from the affirmation or denial of God than from answering any other question'.

Mathematician John Lennox of Oxford University in his book *God's Undertaker: Has Science Buried God?* comments:

When Sir Isaac Newton discovered the universal law of gravitation he did not say 'I have discovered a mechanism that accounts for planetary motion, therefore there is no agent God who designed it'. Quite the opposite: precisely because he understood how it worked, he was moved to increase admiration for the God who had designed it this way ... Theism [belief in God], therefore, upholds and makes sense of the rational intelligibility of the universe ... it is the existence of a Creator that gives to science its fundamental intellectual justification.

God is not going away. The majority of mankind today believes that there is a Supreme Being behind the universe. That's a fact that cannot be denied. The growth of believers world-wide has been phenomenal. For example, adherents to Christian churches in Africa have grown from 10 million in 1900 to over 400 million in 2014 – almost half the total population of the continent. However, there is no denying that Western Europe has become more secular in the past decades, which some are persuaded is a positive boon and others believe a complete disaster.

The idea of God has always been around. In any study of ancient peoples, one can see that religious beliefs were strong among Babylonians, Egyptians, Phoenicians, Assyrians, Greeks and Romans. Where did their religious traditions come from? They did not simply appear out of thin air.

The history of the whole matter is this: the Romans borrowed from Greeks, the Greeks stole from the Egyptians and Phoenicians, while they borrowed from the Chaldeans and Assyrians, who stole from the Abrahamic family all their notions of the spirituality, eternity, and unity of God, the primitive state of man, his fall, sacrifice, priests, altars, immortality of the soul, a future state, eternal judgment and the ultimate retribution of all men according to their works (Alexander Campbell).

The corruption of monotheism (belief in one God) led to polytheism (belief in many gods). Polytheism did not lead to monotheism, as many scholars once believed. 'The same overall picture emerges in studies centred on the traditions of the oldest civilisations known to man: original belief in a "High God", followed by degeneration into polytheism, animism and other corrupt religious notions' (John Blanchard).

Ask yourself, how would someone get to know all about you? Surely one forms the character of a man by what he says and does. It is the same with God. It is from His word and His works we learn of His being and perfection. 'The heavens declare the glory of God; the skies proclaim the work of His hands. Day after day they pour forth speech; night after night they display knowledge' (Psalm 19:1,2). 'Nature attests and displays the knowledge, wisdom, power and goodness of God. The law and the providence of God especially declare His justice, truth and holiness; while the gospel unfolds

His mercy, favour and love; and all these proclaim that God is infinite, eternal and immutable' (Alexander Campbell).

The Bible also refers to the Godhead or Godhood. This is where the Father, Son and Holy Spirit come in – the profoundest of subjects. For example, we read in Genesis: 'Then God said, "Let us make man in our image, after our likeness …"' (1:26a). Please note the plural pronoun. Are there three Gods? No. There is only one true God, but in Him are three personalities in the one nature. What is interesting is that, in man, there are three natures in the one personality. The Bible teaches that body, soul and spirit meet in man and man alone.

A word commonly used for Godhead or Godhood is 'Trinity'. But this term is not found in the Scriptures. In fact, it originated with Tertullian (c. AD 155–220), who used the Latin word *Trinitas*, from which, of course, we get our famous English word. But surely it is best that all should speak of Bible things by Bible words. Using non-Biblical words and the ideas they represent might not be the ideas God wishes to represent. Truly, there is nothing more essential to the unity of all believers or disciples of Christ than the purity of speech.

The Bible teaches that God is, among other things, good, kind, merciful, just, holy, loving, longsuffering, gentle, gracious, meek, patient, righteous, pure, faithful and true. He stands in contrast with Satan (a personality too), who is evil, lying, corrupt, deceitful, proud, false, hateful, slanderous, rebellious and murderous. There is not one chink of light in the character of Satan. There is no darkness or hint of darkness in the character of the Almighty. The contrast could not be clearer.

But God is no pushover. The God of the Bible is not a wishy-washy, namby-pamby character. Neither does He pussy-foot around. If He has to, He can become angry, wrathful and vengeful. He has feelings like everyone else and can be driven only so far. God, in His time, has punished people severely and to the extent of wiping them out. Does that shock you? A lot of people complain at length about how, in the Old Testament, the Amorites were destroyed by God's people, but God's critics too frequently show little interest in the historical background to such events. The truth is that the Amorites had been a wicked people for hundreds of years. Condemning God for his actions against them is like condemning out of hand the Allies of the Second World War for the death and destruction they brought upon the enemy, without regard to the evil they had to overcome.

Ancient people held this view: a nation's God was the greatest and most to be venerated whose people were most successful in battle. God used this commonly held view to the advantage of His chosen nation. In any event, to judge an infant by adult standards is not right. To judge humanity in its infancy by humanity in its maturity is equally not right. It is a true saying that things which might be condoned in one age might not be condoned in another. Don't be quick to judge the Almighty until all the facts are known. After all, 'will not the Judge of all the earth do right?' (Genesis 18:25b).

In this short book it is possible to mention only a little of that which a much greater Book has to tell about the One who loves us and deserves our worship. Hear what the Bible says about God!

I am who I am.

I live forever.

The Lord is the everlasting God, the Creator of the ends of the earth. He will not grow tired or weary, and His understanding no-one can fathom.

His understanding has no limit.

The Lord our God, the Lord is one.

Holy, holy, holy is the Lord God Almighty, who was, and is, and is to come.

Who will not fear you, O Lord, and bring glory to your name? For you alone are holy.

Majestic in holiness, awesome in glory, working wonders.

Great and marvellous are your deeds, Lord God Almighty. Just and true are your ways, King of the nations.

And He passed in front of Moses, proclaiming, 'The Lord, the Lord, the compassionate and gracious God, slow to anger, abounding in love and faithfulness, maintaining love to thousands, and forgiving wickedness, rebellion and sin. Yet He does not leave the guilty unpunished; He punishes the children and their children for the sin of the parents to the third and fourth generation'.

But showing love to a thousand generations of those who love me and keep my commandments.

He is the Rock, His works are perfect, and all His ways are just. A faithful God who does no wrong, upright and just is He.

Now we come to a big question: If there is a God, why then is there so much evil in the world? What is evil anyway? Evil is any destructive force, whether affecting the physical, moral or spiritual realm. There is good in the world and there is also evil in the world. People suffer everywhere because of man's inhumanity to man. But people also suffer as the result of diseases, tsunamis, earthquakes, volcanic eruptions, floods, and so on. Clearly, this world is far from perfect. The Bible tells us why things are as they are. To put it in a nutshell: man fell and nothing has been the same since. The whole universe is damaged goods and that includes mankind. That's why God will one day create a new heaven and a new earth wherein will dwell righteousness (Isaiah 65:17; 66:22; 2 Peter 3:13; Revelation 21:1). So the disease-free, storm-free, sin-free world is in the future. Meanwhile, we have the world that we have – undoubtedly beautiful, but one which is also full of problems, difficulties and imperfections.

Norman L. Geisler's book *If God, Why Evil?* is a most helpful contribution to a troubling subject for many. He writes: '… evil is not a thing in itself, but is a lack or corruption in a good thing. Evil is real – a real lack, a real corruption. But it is not a real thing (substance)'. He points out:

Evil is like a wound in an arm … rot in a tree … rust to a car … moth holes in wool … Heaven is the end and earth is the means. One cannot get to the Promised Land without going through the wilderness. Earth is the testing ground; Heaven is our final home. We cannot reach home without passing through the proving grounds. Allowing the choice of good and evil is necessary in achieving the highest good … One is not fit for the freedom from sin unless he has exercised the freedom to sin, for unless he has had the choice of good over evil, he is not ready for a place where good dominates and evil is defeated. Our initial freedom is designed to lead to the ultimate freedom.

The problem of evil was so great that God had eventually to send His Son into the world to save the world. Satan did everything he could to prevent the Lord entering the world, then, once the Lord was here, he tried to have Him killed, even as a child. But God's plans could not be thwarted. Jesus triumphed in the end, despite persecution and crucifixion. We should take great comfort from the fact that good will ultimately triumph over evil. Mankind has already seen D-Day (Jesus' resurrection from the dead) and VE-Day is assured.

We read in the book of Revelation: 'And the devil, who deceived them, was thrown into the lake of burning sulphur, where the beast and the false prophet had been thrown. They will be tormented day and night for ever and ever' (20:10). We also go on to read in Revelation: 'But the cowardly, the unbelieving, the vile, the murderers, the sexually immoral, those who practise magic arts, the idolaters and all liars – their place will be in the fiery lake of burning sulphur. This is the second death' (21:8). The second death is hell, which was once described by Jesus as 'prepared for the devil and his angels' (Matthew 25:41b). Heaven and hell are words that are bandied about today in all sorts of contexts. But the words speak of real states. They speak of the final destinations of all living souls. Where we spend eternity is up to us. Is it with God and His holy angels or with the devil and his fallen angels?

The God of the Bible is a reality. In fact, He is the ultimate reality. Although unseen by human eyes, He is there and He is not silent. He speaks to us through His written Word. The written Word also records the sayings and doings of the Living Word, who is Jesus, the Son of God and the Saviour of the world. He is worthy of a whole chapter! But before we come to Him, let us consider two simple arguments for the existence of God.

First, the watch argument that William Paley offered in his book: *Paley's Natural Theology*. You find a watch on a heath. You pick it up and inspect it. You see that its several parts are put together for a purpose. The inference is inevitable: the watch must have had a maker. This would also be the case even if the watch is somewhat damaged. You consider the world. You see there is order and complexity in it too. (The human eye is an excellent example.) There is springtime and harvest, summer and winter. The tides continuously ebb and flow. The sun rises and sets each day. Surely, we must come to the same conclusion: the world must also have a Maker.

Second, the rabbit argument by W. Carl Ketcherside:

As for myself, I have examined the available data related to God and revelation and I humbly accept for my own life in simple trusting faith the existence of God and the authenticity and genuineness of His word. When I see rabbit tracks in the newly fallen snow I cannot prove absolutely that the rabbit exists, but I believe that if I patiently follow the tracks I will eventually see the rabbit. There are too many God-tracks on the face of the universe for me to ignore. I'm following them with confident anticipation that some day I shall see Him as He is. Does that strike you as sort of childlike? It is!

# 4  Jesus

The calendar months of July and August are named after the Romans Julius Caesar and his grand-nephew and adopted son Augustus Caesar. Augustus was emperor at the time Jesus was born. These men are big figures in history. Biographies are still being written about them, which proves that Roman history is far from a dead subject.

Adrian Goldsworthy in his book *Caesar* points out that, 'after his death, Caesar was declared a god – the Divine Julius (*divus Julius*) – and his adopted son would style himself the son of a god. However, Augustus himself was not deified in Rome until after his death and this remained the pattern with his successors'. It was deemed by Rome a mark of divinity to change the calendar. The change from BC to AD: was that change not also a mark of divinity – true Divinity?

What is fascinating is that the coming of Jesus in Augustus' day meant that there were two 'Sons of God' on earth at that time, whose goals were identical. Each was dedicated to the task of bringing about universal peace. This would be achieved by the acknowledgement of their sovereignty. So the reality came down to this: the peace of a prince versus the Prince of Peace. Who won in the end? The answer is easy. The Roman empire is long gone, but the kingdom of Christ still stands and, indeed, will stand for ever.

J esus of Nazareth is a historical figure whose existence no historian worth his salt would deny. Tacitus, the famous Roman historian, in his book *The Annals of Imperial Rome* mentions Jesus when describing the famous fire at Rome in the days of Nero and the subsequent persecution of the Christians. He writes:

> To suppress this rumour, Nero fabricated scapegoats – and punished with every refinement the notoriously depraved Christians (as they were popularly called). The originator, Christ, had been executed in Tiberius' reign by the governor of Judaea, Pontius Pilate. But in spite of this temporary setback the deadly superstition had broken out afresh, not only in Judaea (where the mischief had started) but even in Rome.

Another Roman historian, Suetonius, in his book *The Twelve Caesars*, writes about the expulsion of the Jews from Rome during the reign of the emperor Claudius. He says of that emperor: 'He expelled the Jews from Rome, on account of the riots in which they were constantly indulging, at the instigation of Chrestus'. Professor F. F. Bruce in his most helpful work *Jesus & Christian Origins Outside the New Testament* points out that:

> Chrestus, a common slave-name, was a popular mis-spelling of the name of Christ ... the historian appears to have misunderstood the reference to one 'Chrestus' in the police records; he took the reference to mean that this 'Chrestus' was actually in Rome as ringleader of the riotous behaviour in AD 49, but it was in another way that 'Chrestus' became the occasion of these disorders.

Flavius Josephus, the Jewish historian, who was present at the destruction of Jerusalem in AD 70, gives an indirect and a direct reference to Jesus in his large volume known as *Antiquities*. He writes: '... he [Annas, the High Priest] convened a judicial session of the Sanhedrin and brought before it the brother of Jesus the so-called Christ – James by name – and some others, whom he charged with breaking the law and handed over to be stoned to death'. The direct reference reads:

Now, there was about this time Jesus, a wise man, if it be lawful to call him a man, for he was a doer of wonderful works, a teacher of such men as receive the truth with pleasure. He drew over to him both many of the Jews, and many of the Gentiles. He was [the] Christ; and when Pilate, at the suggestion of the principal men amongst us, had condemned him to the cross, those that loved him at the first did not forsake him, for he appeared to them alive again the third day, as the divine prophets had foretold these and ten thousand other wonderful things concerning him; and the tribe of Christians, so named from him, are not extinct to this day.

Undoubtedly, there are modifications here by Christian scribes, but many argue that Josephus' paragraph is not a wholesale interpolation. Professor Bruce agrees. Regrettably, there is insufficient space available to discuss the whole matter in detail.

All in all, 'Josephus bears witness to Jesus' date, to his being the brother of James the Just, to his reputation as a miracle-worker, to his crucifixion under Pilate as a consequence of charges brought against him by the Jewish rulers, to his claim to be the Messiah, and to his being the founder of the "tribe of Christians"' (Bruce).

The story of Jesus is the greatest story ever told. Its impact has been felt everywhere. Has anyone influenced the fields of philosophy, morality, law, music, art, literature, even science, more than Jesus of Nazareth? His influence is worldwide. His adherents today number in excess of two billion. Jesus cannot easily be written off.

The gospel records by Matthew, Mark, Luke and John tell of His life and ministry. They have the ring of truth about them. As we study the life of Jesus, we see the infinite in the finite, the eternal in the temporal, the Divine in the human. Jesus was, simply, *Immanuel*, which means 'God with us'. Why would Matthew, Mark, Luke and John conspire together to tell the world a lie? What was in it for them? Was it the riches, honour, praise and glory of men, or was it humiliation, persecution, privation and suffering? The answer is that these were men who chose to broadcast Christian truth regardless of what it might cost them to do so in a world hostile to their faith.

Let us take John as an example. He was a fisherman turned apostle, just like his brother James. He was much loved by Jesus and was especially close to His Master. He ended up writing the gospel record that bears his name, plus three epistles and the Book of Revelation. The last work was penned while he was banished by the Roman authorities to the island of Patmos in the Aegean Sea.

He became the last surviving apostle on earth and died in his nineties, probably in Ephesus. He had lived through it all – the crucifixion of Jesus, the murder of his brother, the crucifixion of Peter, the death of Paul and the persecution and martyrdom of many of the saints. But nothing deterred him. It is said that towards the end of his life he loved to encourage his fellow-disciples in Ephesus with the words: 'My little children, love one another!' Before he died, he had met head-on the major challenge to the Truth from Gnosticism, one of the greatest '–isms' ever to attack Christianity.

One sect of the Gnostics taught that Jesus was only a phantom. In other words, when He walked about He left no footprints in the ground. John writes: 'That which was from the beginning, which we have heard, which we have seen with our eyes, which we have looked at and our hands have touched – this we proclaim concerning the Word of life' (1 John 1:1). John could hardly have touched a phantom. He gave Jesus the title *Logos* (Word), and to John this had great significance.

John also used *Logos* at the beginning of his gospel record. We read: 'In the beginning was the Word and the Word was with God and the Word was God. He was with God in the beginning. Through Him all things were made; without Him nothing was made that has been made. In Him was life, and that life was the light of men' (John 1:1-4). Then, a few sentences later, he wrote: 'The Word became flesh and made His dwelling among us. We have seen His glory, the glory of the Only Begotten, who came from the Father, full of grace and truth' (1:14). To the ancients the term *Logos* meant reason as well as word. So what John is saying is that the mind of God became a person of flesh and blood – Jesus of Nazareth. William Barclay has written: 'So John went out to the Jews and Greeks to tell them that in Jesus Christ this creating, illuminating, controlling, sustaining mind of God had come to earth. He came to tell them that men need no longer guess and grope; all that they had to do was to look at Jesus and see the mind of God'.

As mentioned in the chapter on the Bible, John also wrote of the importance of miracles and the account given of them (John 20:30,31). And so this is as good a place as any to touch upon the subject of miracles and, especially, the miracles of Christ. But what is a miracle? Some answers given are:

Miracles are but special acts of God's will.

A miracle is a display of supernatural power in attestation of the truth of a message from God.

Miracles are simply the application of Divine power upon a higher level or plane.

Miracles are of two kinds; namely, of fore-knowledge and of power. The resurrection of a dead man is a miracle of power; but to foretell the resurrection is a miracle of fore-knowledge.

Jesus performed miracles throughout His ministry. What else would we expect? Surely a man claiming to be the promised Messiah and the Son of God must have had the ability to foretell events, heal the sick, cast out demons, raise the dead, calm storms, turn water into wine, feed multitudes from two loaves and five fishes, and more. Jesus did not perform these deeds to prove He was the Son of God but because such acts were a part of His being. John's task was to record certain of Jesus' miracles to show us that He was indeed the Son of God.

Books have been written to explain the miracles of Jesus and books have been written to explain them away. What we should do is simply accept them and glory in them, and from them learn that there is in the universe a power superior to the laws of nature. The purpose of miracles is not to save, but to make credible the claims of Jesus to be the Christ, the Son of God. No one today can deny Jesus' miracles. It is too late for that. All people can do now is to doubt the witnesses, or question the evidence.

Many people in the world today believe only in naturalism. Naturalism means there is nature and nothing else but nature. In the famous words of Carl Sagan: 'The cosmos is all there is, or was, or ever shall be'. The American lawyer, Phillip E. Johnson, in his book *Testing Darwinism* says that to him 'there is no difference between naturalism and materialism'. Those who believe only in naturalism or materialism discount completely supernaturalism. John Lennox has written: '... the real battle is not so much between science and faith in God, but rather between a materialistic, or more broadly, a naturalistic world-view and a supernaturalistic, or theistic, worldview'. Jesus showed quite clearly there is a supernatural realm. He came from there. He broke into the space-time continuum by way of the incarnation and after His resurrection He returned to heaven. From there He now reigns as King of Kings and Lord of Lords (Revelation 19:16). All authority has been given to Him both in heaven and on earth (Matthew 28:18). His kingdom is in this world, but not of it. That's what He told Pilate ( John 18:36) and that's what all His disciples believe.

Jesus said many wonderful things during His time on earth. Asked by His disciple Thomas, '"Lord, we don't know where you are going, so how can we know the way?" Jesus answered: "I am the Way and the Truth and the Life. No-one comes to the Father except through me. If you really knew me, you would know my Father as well. From now on you do know Him and have seen Him"' ( John 14:5-7).

The early believers were known as the people of 'the Way'. Christianity is not so much a way of life, but Life in the Way, who is a person – Christ

Jesus. It's interesting that Jesus spoke about two ways. In Matthew we read: 'Enter through the narrow gate. For wide is the gate and broad is the way that leads to destruction, and many enter through it. But small is the gate and narrow is the way that leads to life, and only a few find it' (7:13,14). Note, one way or road leads to destruction, and the other, to life. The former is broad, not because God designed it so, but because the vast majority walks in it. The latter is narrow, not because God designed it so, but because so few have found it. The fact that it has to be found means that no one is ever going to stumble into it. But where is it to be found? Jesus' answer could not be clearer: 'I am the Way'. The reality is that every human being on earth is either in the one way or the other. Such a contrast is not unusual in the Bible. In the Good Book, it's saint and sinner, truth and falsehood, right and wrong, light and darkness, righteousness and sinfulness, virtue and vice, wisdom and folly, life and death, heaven and hell. There are many others.

There is a proverb found in the Bible that provides us with a stark warning. It says: 'There is a way that seems right to a man, but in the end it leads to death' (Proverbs 14:12; 16:25). In the U.K. not all roads lead to London. If a driver is heading from

Glasgow, Scotland to the great capital and sees a sign 'Aberdeen – 100 miles', then he knows he's on the wrong road. He's heading north, not south. If he continues on this road then he has no hope of reaching London. What he must do is stop, turn around, get on the road to England and take it from there. People in the broad way have to do the same. They must stop, turn around or convert (Latin: *con* plus *vertere*, which mean 'to turn together with') and get on the narrow road that leads to life. In other words, the sinner must admit he is lost and turn to Jesus for salvation.

Jesus is also the Truth. Francis Bacon, in one of his famous essays, wrote: 'What is truth? said jesting Pilate; and would not stay for an answer'. The encounter between Jesus and Pilate is found in John's Gospel chapter 18. The great tragedy for Pilate was that the Truth was standing right in front of him and in the end, under great pressure from the religious leaders of the Jews, he condemned the Truth to death. One day for Pilate the tables will be turned and he will stand before the judgment seat of Christ with everyone else. But the difference will be that, on the great day, Jesus will judge in righteousness. The righteous will not be condemned and the guilty will not go free. Justice will be done!

When Jesus said He was the Truth, He was saying He was the Reality. Jesus is the only real person who has lived in this world. That is, He is the only person about whom there was never any sham or pretence. He was the sinless One, the perfect One, the Son of the Living God. So Jesus not only spoke the truth, but was the embodiment of it.

It is important to make clear what is meant by saying that Jesus spoke and embodied truth:

> Truth is agreement with, or conformity to, reality in whatever area is being considered. When we speak of scientific truths we refer only to that which has been verified and indisputably established. When we speak of moral truths we refer to those teachings which are in exact harmony with the ethical or moral values which have been established by proper authority for the wellbeing of humanity (W. Carl Ketcherside).

Please note there is a difference between truth and fact. Truth is that which is; fact is that which is done.

There are many statements about truth worth repeating. Here are a few of them:

Truth is not affected by time or place.

Every honest heart will at once embrace and adopt all known truth.

Truth has nothing to fear from investigation.

All truth is harmonious and consistent. One truth cannot contradict another truth.

No pleasure is comparable to standing on the vantage ground of truth.

Truth is a capital virtue without which there is no goodness in man.

Truth is the basis of all confidence amongst rational human beings ... unbelief and mistrust are the natural results of a system of lying and deceit.

All truth is equally true, but not all truth is equally important.

The overall importance of truth can be seen in the oath sworn in a court of law: 'I swear to tell the truth, the whole truth, and nothing but the truth, so help me God'. However, too often nowadays, the court hears anything but the truth. To lie is of Satan. Jesus once said of Satan that he 'is a liar and the father of lies' (John 8:44b). Liars will one day be condemned to the second death (Revelation 21:8).

God is Truth. He is Absolute Truth. We say this despite the fact that many people today believe that all truth is relative. In other words, what is true for you might not be true for me. Relativism is the inevitable result of believing in fallible man above an infallible God.

Jesus is Truth. He is Absolute Truth. That makes Him a unique Prophet, Priest and King.

In addition, Jesus spells Life. Not only is Jesus the originator of physical life, he also the source of spiritual or eternal life. He once said: 'I have come that they may have life and  have it to the full' (John 10:10b). That assumes that people are dead, and indeed they are – dead in trespasses and sins. Truly, a person can be alive and dead at the same time. In other words, a person can be physically alive and yet spiritually dead to God. People need to be resurrected from the dead and Jesus can perform this deed by their being obedient to His gospel call.

The resurrection of Jesus of Nazareth from the

dead is the greatest fact of all time. If Jesus did not rise from the dead then the faith of every Christian in the world is futile (1 Corinthians 15:14). But He did triumph over the grave, as prophesied by others and by Himself, and reported by witnesses.

Jesus of Nazareth is the only person in the history of the world to die, be resurrected, and die no more. It is recorded that He Himself had raised three people during His ministry – Jairus' daughter (Matthew 9:18-26; Mark 5:35-43; Luke 8:49-56), the widow's son at Nain (Luke 7:11-17), and Lazarus (John 11:38-44). But, of course, all three later died again. We read that Jesus, forty days after His resurrection, ascended to heaven (Acts 1:9) from where He reigns over His eternal kingdom. In heaven He was crowned King of Kings and Lord of Lords (Revelation 19:16). So Jesus is no dead Saviour. He is a Living Lord.

Life is union; death is separation. All living things are alive because of their union with nature. Separate that union and death takes place. For example, there is all the difference in the world between a living tree and a dead piece of wood. But what makes a human being alive? The Bible reveals that in the human being there is the union of body, soul and spirit. Break that union and death takes place. James once wrote: 'As the body without the spirit is dead, so faith without deeds is dead' (James 2:26).

But, there is life and there is the more abundant life. This is where the Spirit of God comes in. He, like Jesus, is a personality of the Godhead. The apostle Paul once wrote: 'And if the Spirit of Him who raised Jesus from the dead is living in you, He who raised Christ from the dead will also give life to your mortal bodies through His Spirit, who lives in you' (Romans 8:11). When does the Spirit come to dwell with us? In short, He comes at our baptism. But more of that later.

Life and death – what a subject! Life is positive; death is negative. In fact, the apostle Paul once described death as an enemy (1 Corinthians 15:26). But life, not death, will triumph in the end. One day, death will be destroyed for ever. In heaven, amongst many things, there will be no more death (Revelation 21:4). That's the life!

# 5 The Spirit of God

When Jesus returned to heaven, He promised to send His Spirit as a Comforter to His disciples. They needed all the help they could get in living in this world and in taking the name of Jesus to the world, first to the Jews, then to the Gentiles. That support came by way of the Spirit. We read that Jesus said: 'If you love Me, you will obey what I command. And I will ask the Father and He will give you another Comforter to be with you forever – the Spirit of truth' (John 14:15-17a). He also told His apostles: 'But when He, the Spirit of truth comes, He will guide you into all truth ...' (John 16:13a). 'All truth' does not refer here to the truth related to all aspects of the universe, but the truth that redeems and restores the Divine-human relationship.

The Greek word that has been translated as comforter – capitalised above because there it is used of a personality of the Godhead - is an interesting one. It is *parakletos* and means, literally, called to one's side, i.e., to one's aid. 'It was used in a court of justice to denote a legal assistant, counsel for the defence, an advocate; then, generally, one who pleads another's cause, an intercessor, advocate ... In the widest sense, it signifies a succourer, comforter' (W. E. Vine). The Greek original for the word 'another' is equally interesting. It is *allos* and means another of the same kind. It is not *heteros*, which means another of a different kind. So Jesus sent the Spirit, who is like Himself who could encourage, support and strengthen all believers in the age during which He was absent. Granted, all disciples possess the gift of the Spirit, but they do not possess the gifts of the Spirit so evident, for example, in the Corinthian church. In fact, the Corinthians did not lack any spiritual gift (1 Corinthians 1:7). In 1 Corinthians chapters 12-14 it is revealed that they had such gifts as prophecy, healing, performing miracles, speaking in tongues and interpreting tongues. These constituted the scaffolding for the building of the church. Once the church was completed and in place then the scaffolding was no longer required and, therefore, removed.

Please remember that the early church did not have the complete written revelation from God as we have today. Thus the church required special powers of the Spirit to guide it until the glorious secrets of God were fully declared. Pay careful attention to what Paul said at the conclusion of the Roman letter:

Now to Him who is able to establish you by my gospel and the proclamation of Jesus Christ, according to the revelation of the mystery hidden for long ages past, but now revealed and made known through the prophetic writings by the command of the eternal God, so that all nations might believe and obey Him – to the only wise God be glory for ever through Jesus Christ! Amen (Romans 16:25-27).

There are seven functions of the Holy Spirit. He has operated or operates in these following areas:

Creation
Revelation
Incarnation
Inspiration
Confirmation
Corporation
Transformation

Let us briefly consider them all.

*Creation.* It was the Spirit who brought order out of chaos. The first two verses of the Bible say: 'In the beginning God created the heavens and the earth. Now the earth was formless and empty, darkness was over the surface of the deep, and the Spirit of God was hovering over the waters' (Genesis 1:1,2). The Spirit is also involved in the 'new creation' of those who have turned to Christ: 'Therefore, if anyone is in Christ, he is a new creation; the old has gone, the new has come!' (2 Corinthians: 5:17).

*Revelation.* The Spirit helped produce the written revelation from God. On the subject of prophecy, for example, we have these words by Peter: 'For prophecy never had its origin in the will of man, but men spoke from God as they were carried along by the Holy Spirit' (2 Peter 1:21). Paul wrote: 'However, as it is written: "No eye has seen, nor ear heard, no mind has conceived what God has prepared for those who love Him" – but God has revealed it to us by His Spirit' (1 Corinthians 2:9,10).

*Incarnation.* The Holy Spirit was involved in the conception of Jesus. It was He who impregnated Mary. We read: 'This is how the birth of Jesus Christ came about: His mother Mary was pledged to be married to Joseph, but before they came together, she was found to be with child through the Holy Spirit' (Matthew 1:18). We came into the world by procreation, but Jesus by incarnation. Many people today say they have a problem with the virgin birth. What they actually doubt is not the virgin birth, but the virgin conception. But why should anyone question the ability of the Supreme Being to fertilise an ovum within Mary? He who created the whole procreative system could easily intervene at any stage for His own purposes.

*Inspiration.* We have already touched on this subject under the Bible. Inspiration is the method God chose to ensure that His word is transmitted to each succeeding generation. The Bible is a living book and is the instrument to produce the more abundant life in all sinners. It is a book pointing us to Jesus – the great Life-giver and the great Life-sustainer.

*Confirmation.* The truth about Jesus, for example, was the subject of confirmation. All truth must be made credible before the human mind can accept it – natural truths by natural phenomena, supernatural truths by supernatural phenomena or miracles. We read in Hebrews: 'This salvation which was first announced by the Lord, was confirmed to us by those who heard Him. God also testified to it by signs, wonders and various miracles, and gifts of the Holy Spirit distributed according to His will' (2:3b-4). The gospel of Mark concludes thus: 'After the Lord Jesus had spoken to them, He was taken up into heaven and He sat at the right hand of God. Then the disciples went out and preached everywhere, and the Lord worked with them and confirmed His word by the signs that accompanied it' (16:19,20). Truth once confirmed never needs to be confirmed again. The testimony of the apostles is still valid despite their deaths long ago.

*Corporation.* The church is described by Paul as a body. 'The body is a unit, though it is made up of many parts; and though all its parts are many, they form one body. So it is with Christ. For we were all baptised by one Spirit into one body – whether Jews or Greeks, slave or free – and we were all given the one Spirit to drink' (1 Corinthians 12:12,13). There is only one body. There never has been any more than one. Every saved person in the world is in the body of Christ. Today, many a Christian will say that he or she is a member of a church. But is it not more accurate to say that he or she is a member of the body of Christ?

*Transformation.* The Spirit transforms the life of all true believers. In Him, hate can turn to love. Paul wrote, 'And hope does not disappoint us, because God has poured out His love into our hearts by the Holy Spirit, whom He has given us' (Romans 5:5). The desire of all disciples is to be more Christlike as day succeeds day. Jesus is our perfect example. If we measure our lives against Him then we cannot go wrong. Any other measurement is imperfect. We need the power of the Spirit to see us through in this mixed-up mess and messed-up mix of a world. In such a world there are manifestations of a spirit that would seek to lead us astray, but as the apostle John has written: 'You, dear children, are from God and have overcome them, because the One who is in you is greater than the one [Satan] who is in the world' (1 John 4:4).

Paul in his letter to the Galatians gives us a contrast – a contrast between the fruit of the Spirit and the works of the flesh or the acts of sinful human nature. He says:

> The acts of the sinful nature are obvious: sexual immorality, impurity and debauchery; idolatry and witchcraft; hatred, discord, jealousy, fits of rage, selfish ambition, dissensions, factions and envy; drunkenness, orgies, and the like. I warn

you, as I did before, that those who live like this will not inherit the kingdom of God. But the fruit of the Spirit is love, joy, peace, patience, kindness, goodness, faithfulness, gentleness and temperance. Against such things there is no law (Galatians 5:19-23).

There is much to study here. Love in the Greek in which the New Testament was originally written is *agape*. This love concerns the will as well as the heart. It has everything to do with unconquerable benevolence. 'It means no matter what a man does to you by way of insult or injury or humiliation we will never seek anything else but his highest good' (William Barclay).

Joy is *chara* and occurs sixty times in the New Testament. The verb *charein*, which means to rejoice, occurs seventy-two times. So we can see that the New Testament is a book of joy. Paul once wrote, 'Rejoice in the Lord always. I will say it again: Rejoice!' (Philippians 4:4): this not just any joy, but a joy whose foundation is in the Lord.

Peace is *eirene* (hence the name Irene) and has everything to do with what makes for a man's highest good. The equivalent word in Hebrew is *shalom*. Peace is far more than freedom from trouble or cessation of hostility. 'It describes the serenity, the tranquillity, the perfect contentment of the life which is completely happy and secure' (Barclay).

Patience is *makrothumia* and means long-tempered. T. K. Abbot says it is 'the self-restraint which does not retaliate a wrong'. Another writer says it is 'the forbearance which endures injuries and evil deeds without being provoked to anger or revenge'. The brilliant linguist, Richard C. Trench, once said of *makrothumia*: 'A long holding out of the mind, before it gives room to action or passion'. We see in the word God's own longsuffering to fallen mankind.

Kindness is *chrestotes*. There is a certain mellowness in this word. It is a kindness that has in it a gracious, personal, warm effectiveness. In other words, it is not a vague, nebulous emotion, but an emotion fully engaged in the world. Kindness really involves treating others as God treats us.

Goodness is *agathosune* (hence the name Agatha) and has to do with a strong goodness. It is a goodness that can rebuke and discipline. The primary idea in the word is generosity – a generosity that springs from a heart that is kind.

Faithfulness is *pistis* and the word speaks of one who is reliable and trustworthy. 'It describes the man on whose faithful service we may rely, on whose loyalty we may depend, whose word we can unreservedly accept. It describes the man in whom there is the unswerving and inflexible fidelity of Jesus Christ and the utter dependability of God' (Barclay).

Gentleness or meekness is *prautes*. It is a word that speaks of strength under control. Alexander the Great had a horse, Bucephalus, whom many thought could never be tamed. But the young Alexander defied all the odds and eventually trained Bucephalus to be subject to the bit. This great horse later proved its worth in battle after battle. A well-known definition of *prautes* is: always angry at the right time and never angry at the wrong time. Yes, there is such a thing as righteous indignation! It is good to have self-control, but there is even better than that – God-control.

Temperence is *enkrateia* and means self-restraint. The verb *kratein* means to grip, grasp, hold, control. The man who has a controlling grip of himself can control others. Too often we read today of people being out of control. The indwelling Spirit of God brings discipline to everyone's life. We need His strength to overcome our weaknesses and to overcome our adversary, the devil, who is ever out to tempt and destroy.

Someone once said: 'To walk after the flesh is the fate of once-born men. To walk after the Spirit is the feat of twice-born men'. The New Testament Scriptures tell us Christians must walk in newness of life; after the Spirit; in honesty; by faith; in good works; in love; in wisdom; in truth; and after the commandments of the Lord. In other words, there is plenty to be getting on with. The kingdom of God is no place for idleness.

# 6 Humanity

Who am I? Why am I here? Where am I going? What does it mean to be human? What makes you different from your pet dog or cat? The Bible, of course, answers all of these questions; but, sadly, many remain in the dark and are still seeking and searching for meaning in their lives outside the Scriptures.

The modern existentialist, for example, says that, ultimately, there is no meaning to life. The famous saying is: 'The meaning of man is that man is meaningless'. So, for many today, man is dead. As Francis Schaeffer has written: 'Man has no meaning, no purpose, no significance. There is only pessimism concerning man as man ... The note of desperation is reflected in the Theatre of the Absurd ... Man is a tragic joke in a context of total cosmic absurdity ... The Bible teaches that though man is hopelessly lost, he is not nothing'. Schaeffer is, perhaps, thinking of the title of the famous book by the existentialist Jean Paul Sartre – *Being and Nothingness*. To read it is to end up more confused than before.

Existentialism is just one subject in the vast field of philosophy. Both Christians and those of other faiths or none have written philosophy, but we might wonder if philosophers who have produced their works uninspired by the wisdom of God can truly add to the wisdom of man. Of course, they doubtless meant well. Karl Marx, for example, wished to improve the lot of man. But whether the millions who starved or were murdered in the various reigns of terror conducted by Stalin, Mao Tse-tung and their lesser imitators would judge him to have succeeded, we may reasonably doubt. Anyone who reads *The Black Book of Communism: Crimes, Terror, Repression* by a group of French scholars will find it a complete eye-opener to a godless political system.

Philosophy does deal with the big questions, but through man's wisdom, not God's. It is the history of the thought processes of men throughout the ages. The age of doubting is the era of philosophy. Men never began to produce hypotheses till they lost their way. Someone once said: 'Philosophy, at best, is but the reason or wisdom of man, while the Bible is both the reason and wisdom of God'. John Buchan kept philosophy in its proper place. He knew it did not provide the final answer to the meaning of life. He wrote: 'Philosophy was to me an intellectual exercise, like mathematics, not the quest for a faith'.

True wisdom is found in the Bible. The Bible reveals clearly to us that men and women are made in the image of God and this distinguishes them from all animals. Human beings do have an animal body and an animal soul, but that part of them which marks them as being in the image of God lies in their intellectual, moral and religious spirit. The spirit has the faculties we call the powers of understanding; the soul has its passions and affections; the body has its organs and their funct-ions. Martin Luther once wrote: 'The spirit is the highest and noblest part of man, which qualifies him to lay hold of the incomprehensible, invisible, exter-nal things; in short, it is the house where faith and God's word are at home'. W. Carl Ketcherside put it this way:

Within this tenement of clay called the body, dwells a spirit. God has 'formed the spirit of man within him' (Zechariah 12:1). That spirit is the inward man which can be renewed daily, even while the outward man perishes (2 Cor-inthians 4:16). It is strengthened with might in the Holy Spirit (Ephesians 3:16). It is the spirit, held captive in the body, which longs and groans for the day of adoption when the body shall have redemption (Romans 8:23). It is the spirit, confined to an alien realm, which aspires to a higher sphere; which yearns and gropes and reaches out to embrace its Creator, and to know again the bliss of perfect union which was so rudely shattered by sin.

John C. Whitcomb in his book *The Early Earth* highlights the uniqueness of the human being in the world. He says:

Of living beings on this planet, only man is self-conscious as a person; is sufficiently free from the bondage of instinct to exercise real choices and to have significant purposes and goals in life; has complex emotions including sadness and joy; appreciates art and music creatively; can make real tools; can be truly educated rather than merely trained; can use oral and written symbols to communicate abstract concepts to other persons and thus enjoy true fellowship; can accumulate knowledge and attain wisdom beyond previous generations and thus make genuine history; can discern moral right from wrong and suffer agonies of conscience; can recognise the existence and rightful demands of His Creator through worship, sacrifice, and religious service. Only man will exist forever as a personal being either in heaven or hell.

Human beings are moral beings. Can that be said of monkeys, apes or peacocks? The scientist, Professor Edgar H. Andrews in his book *Who Made God?* says that 'man appears to be the only creature that can distinguish between "right" and "wrong"'. He goes on to speak of 'the fact of human moral awareness … atheists argue that morality is an evolutionary phenomenon that arose because it has survival value. But quite apart from the difficulty of fashioning the silk purse of morality from the sow's ear of evolution, this is contrary to all the evidence'. Andrews is one of the great critics of the theory of evolution. He is not alone. For example, the website *Dissent from Darwin* contains the names of scores of scientists, who are either highly critical of the theory or who reject it entirely. Amoeba to man is a story and a half, but that's another book!

John Blanchard has written:

If the universe is no more than matter, energy, time and chance, how can 'right' and 'wrong' have any meaning? How can we derive personal morality from a fundamentally impersonal universe? ... How can we jump from molecules to morality? How can we explain concepts of good and evil in mechanistic terms? In an atheistic universe with no moral obligations, and in which human beings are merely shrink-wrapped bags of biological elements governed by the laws of physics, where can we find any basis for exercising moral judgment about anything? How could an impersonal reality make me feel any moral obligation to be honest, kind or truthful?

Some scientists today believe that science has all the answers, even in morality. In other words, there is no truth but scientific truth. The humanist philosopher Alister J. Sinclair has pointed out: 'The more assiduously that scientists defend science against all comers, the more their beliefs become indistinguishable from religious beliefs. Their beliefs become "scientism" which is a philosophy instead of science'.

How can science tell you if a poem is good or bad? How can science tell you if a painting is good

71

or bad? How can science tell you what is right and wrong? As John Lennox has said: 'Science can tell you that, if you add strychnine to someone's drink, it will kill them. But science cannot tell you whether it is morally right or wrong to put strychnine into your grandmother's tea so that you can get your hands on her property'. There are limits to science. It doesn't have all the answers.

For others, it is law that keeps people moral. But does it? As Judge Patrick Devlin points out in his 1965 book *The Enforcement of Morals*:

The law cannot make people good; it can only punish them for being bad or at least discourage them … Society cannot live without morals. Its morals are those standards of conduct which the reasonable man approves … No society has yet solved the problem of how to teach morality without religion. So the law must base itself on Christian morals and to the limit of its ability enforce them, not simply because they are the morals of most of us, nor simply because they are the morals which are taught by the established Church – on these points the law recognises the right to dissent – but for the compelling reason that without the help of Christian teaching the law will fail.

Devlin's book is a challenging read, but a rewarding one. He cuts across the thinking of many today. For example, he says: 'Not everything is to be tolerated. No society can do without intolerance, indignation and disgust; they are the forces behind the moral law …'

Can you be moral without the Christian religion? Of course. People existed as moral beings for a long time before Jesus came. There was ethics before Christian ethics. Even heathen philosophers could discover moral truths. After all, moral truths have always been present in the world. God was not silent in the past. If he had been then how, for example, did a Job, an Abraham or a Joseph know how to live rightly in His sight?

But Jesus offers more than a moral code. Christianity is not an ethical code trying to make us good from without, but an inner transformation, which purifies from within. Let it be emphasised again that we all need the power within – the indwelling Spirit. It is He who brings life, the more abundant life or eternal life. It is through Him that we can crucify the deeds of sinful human nature. It is through Him we can be truly human and truly happy.

# 7  Sin and salvation

The writer G. K. Chesterton once remarked: 'Whatever else is true of man, man is not what he was meant to be'. No one is perfect. The Good Book says: 'As it is written: "There is no-one righteous, not even one ..."' (Romans 3:10) and '... for all have sinned and fall short of the glory of God ...' (Romans 3:23).

What is sin? Alexander Cruden in his *Complete Concordance to the Old and New Testaments* says that it is 'any thought, word, action, omission, or desire, contrary to the law of God'. *The Shorter Oxford English Dictionary* defines sin as 'a transgression against the divine law and an offence against God'. *Webster's Dictionary* says of the verb: 'To depart voluntarily from the path of duty prescribed by God to man; to violate the divine law in any particular'. Synonyms for the noun are: wrongdoing, iniquity, violation, offence, misdeed, ungodliness, trespass, wickedness, transgression, vice, and many more. All of them paint a bad picture.

One of the Hebrew words for sin is *avon* and is usually translated 'iniquity'. Another one is *pesha* and it speaks of sin as 'rebellion'. Rebellion comes from the Latin word *bellum*, meaning war. Sin always causes war, even within the individual.

Revelation chapter 12 speaks to us of a war in heaven. We read: '... Michael and his angels fought against the dragon, and the dragon and his angels fought back. But he was not strong enough, and they lost their place in heaven. The great dragon was hurled down – that ancient serpent called the devil or Satan, who leads the whole world astray. He was hurled to the earth, and his angels with him' (7-9). Peter also refers to the result of this war, when he writes: 'For if God did not spare angels when they sinned, but sent them to hell [Greek: *Tartarus*] putting them into gloomy dungeons [some manuscripts read 'into chains of darkness'] to be held for judgment ...' (2 Peter 2:4). The fallen angels are probably the demons about which we read so much in the gospel records.

So war began in heaven, not on earth, and the consequences of this war of all wars are still with us. The casualties are enormous. Satan is trying to take down as many people as possible with him. Hell

75

or Gehenna awaits him and his angels. Jesus once said of this hell or eternal fire that it is 'prepared for the devil and his angels' (Matthew 25:41b). We should read His words carefully within their context because Jesus reveals that Gehenna will also be the destination for all unrepentant sinners who appear before His judgment throne, standing to His left (25:41-46). Jesus is not speaking here about a fantasy, but a reality. Jesus has provided a way to escape from the power, pollution and domination of sin; escape also from the punishment for sin. That way of escape is through Him. His willingness to come into this world to suffer and die on a cross reveals His wonderful love for us all and His full awareness of the dreadful fate that awaits us if we do not accept the salvation offered.

There is a war within as well as a war without. Both James and Peter talk about the lusts which war against the soul (James 4:1,2; 1 Peter 2:11). Plato saw this war within as a conflict between the demands of the passions and the control of reason. He knew that something dramatic was taking place in his life, and indeed there was. Jesus and His disciples reveal just how dramatic it is. The Lord said on one occasion: 'For from within, out of men's hearts, come evil thoughts, sexual immorality, theft, murder, adultery, greed, malice, deceit, lewdness, envy, slander, arrogance, and folly. All these evils come from inside and make a man "unclean"' (Mark 7:20-23). It was the Scottish poet Robert Burns who wrote:

> The heart aye's the part aye
> That makes us right or wrang.
>
> [The heart's always the part
> That makes us right or wrong.]

Truly, at the heart of most human problems today is the problem of the human heart.

What does the Bible tells us about the heart? First, it tells us that the heart has to do with the intellect. The heart thinks, understands, knows, believes, doubts, ponders, reasons and judges. Second, the heart has to do with the emotions and sensibilities. We love with the heart; we despise with the heart. The heart is the seat of gladness and sorrow. Love, joy, wonder, admiration, fear and hate are all emotions of the heart. Third, the heart has to do with the will. We determine with the heart; purpose with the heart; repent with the heart and obey from the heart.

To clean up our life, we have to clean out our heart. This is where Jesus comes in. Jesus is in the cleansing business – and how!

The main Greek noun for sin is *hamartia*. This was originally a shooting word. It described what happened when a shot arrow or a hurled javelin missed the target. 'Sin is the failure to be what we should have been and what we ought to have been, what we could have been and what we might have been' (William Barclay). Other Greek words emphasise sin as transgression; stumbling through lack of care; lawlessness; ungodliness; unrighteousness; and failure of duty to God. In the verb forms: to refuse to hear, to ignore, and to disobey.

Sin has resulted in physical death, spiritual death and the danger of eternal death. So sin and death are inextricably linked. Paul once described death as an enemy. He said to the Corinthians: 'The last enemy to be destroyed is death' (1 Corinthians 15:26).

Clearly, the Bible teaches that someone can be alive and yet dead at the same time. Someone can be physically alive and yet spiritually dead. Paul said: 'But the widow who lives for pleasure is dead even while she lives' (1 Timothy 5:6). The hedonists of this world are dead as far as God is concerned. For sure, they travel to places like Ibiza in the Mediterranean Sea to have 'a good time' or 'get stoned' or engage in 'free sex'. These people should be ashamed to live and afraid to die. They need to turn their world around. They need to be resurrected from the dead, as do all sinners. Let them recall the words of the loving father to the prodigal son when he returned home: 'For this son of mine was dead and is alive again; he was lost and is found' (Luke 15:24). The heavenly Father wants all sinners to do the same. He wants them to return home – home with Him. But what must we do to be saved? Let us now attempt to answer this question.

Paul wrote: 'Here is a trustworthy saying that deserves full acceptance: Christ Jesus came into the world to save sinners – of whom I am the worst' (1 Timothy 1:15). We read in John's gospel: 'For God did not send His Son into the world to condemn the world, but to save the world through Him' (3:17). Paul also wrote: 'Grace and peace to you from God our Father and the Lord Jesus Christ, who gave Himself for our sins to rescue us from the present evil age, according to the will of our God and Father, to whom be glory for ever and ever. Amen' (Galatians 1:3-5). So Jesus is all about salvation.

'Salvation – it is to make an ignorant being intelligent; a polluted one pure; a sinful one obedient; and a despairing one hopeful and joyous' (Isaac Erret).

There are two sides to salvation: the Divine and the human. The Divine part is what is expressed by the word *grace*. The human part is expressed by the word *faith*.

God gradually worked out His plans and purposes over a long period. We read of them in the Old Testament. There He is revealed as a covenant-making God. We read about the covenant with Noah; the covenant with Abraham; and the so-called old covenant or testament given through Moses. Now God has given us a new covenant in Christ Jesus. Clearly, God has chosen to relate to man on the basis of covenants and God's covenants with man are always acts of Divine grace.

A simple covenant is an agreement between two parties. Both are equal in the eyes of the law. But in a Divine-human covenant the parties are not equal. God stands supreme. He proposes and man accepts.

The covenant given through Moses was a covenant of law. Why was the Law given? It was given as a pedagogue (in its original sense – a slave who led a boy to school) to lead us to Christ (Galatians 3:24). The Law was perfect, but the trouble was, and is, that human beings are not. No one can be saved by keeping a law. All need to be saved by a Saviour. When the time was right, God didn't send us another law like the Law of Moses, but He sent us His Son. Salvation or forgiveness of sins is now through obedience to Him.

Jesus' covenant is a covenant of grace. Grace is the undeserved generosity of God. Grace is God's unmerited favour. Divine grace reached its apex in Christ. 'Grace is the God who is love, giving up glory and moving into the human sphere, being tested, tempted, tried, agonising and sorrowing and then triumphing over the human predicament and offering me not a hand-out or even a hand-up, but taking me in His own arms, whispering to me that in Him I am safe evermore' (W. Carl Ketcherside).

The gospel or good news of Christ is for all. Paul said to Titus: 'For the grace of God that brings salvation has appeared to all men' (Titus 2:11). Jesus, after His resurrection, told His apostles, 'Go into all the world and preach the good news to all creation' (Mark 16:15). Paul later wrote: 'I am not ashamed of the gospel because it is the power of God for the salvation of everyone who believes: first for the Jew, then for the Gentile' (Romans 1:16). The gospel is the good news of Jesus.

Paul declared to the Corinthians: 'For what I received I passed on to you as of first importance: that Christ died for our sins according to the Scriptures, that He was buried, that He was raised on the third day according to the Scriptures ...' (1 Corinthians 15:3,4). As the first covenant was sealed in blood so the New Covenant is sealed in the blood of Jesus – the true 'Lamb of God who takes away the sin of the world' (John 1:29b). In Hebrews we read: '... without the shedding of blood there is no forgiveness' (Hebrews 9:22b).

Sacrifice is as old as the Fall and was first commanded by God. The killing of all those innocent animals in the patriarchal and Jewish dispensations 'could not and did not take away sin. They were but types of the real sacrifice ... Christ's death is, therefore, a real and all-sufficient sacrifice for sin and stands in the attitudes of propitiation, reconciliation, expiation, and redemption; from which spring to us justification, sanctification, adoption and eternal life' (Alexander Campbell). Campbell in his outstanding book *The Christian System* goes on to point out that the sacrifice of Christ 'is, indeed, infinite in value, as respects the expiation of sin, or its propitiatory power; but as respects the actual reconciliation and redemption of sinners, it is limited to those only who believe and obey the gospel'.

The vital importance of belief and obedience can be seen in the following passages: 'Whoever believes and is baptised will be saved, but whoever does not believe will be condemned' (Mark 16:16). 'And without faith it is impossible to please God, because anyone who comes to Him must believe that He exists and that He rewards those who earnestly seek Him' (Hebrews 11:6). 'God is just: He will pay back trouble to those who trouble you and give relief to you who are troubled, and to us as well. This will happen when the Lord Jesus is revealed from heaven in blazing fire with His powerful angels. He will punish those who do not know God and do not obey the gospel of our Lord Jesus' (2 Thessalonians 1:6-8).

A study of the New Testament book Acts of the Apostles reveals how sinners were saved in the early days of Christianity. Nothing has changed. What they did to be saved then we must do to be saved now.

The apostle Peter laid out what we have to do. In Acts 2 we have the record of the first ever gospel address. It was Peter who delivered it to his fellow Jews. His action came as no surprise because it was to Peter that Jesus gave the keys of the kingdom (Matthew 16:19). Keys are for opening doors and Peter used the keys, first, to open the door of the kingdom to the Jews and, second, to the Gentiles (Acts 10). What happened to these keys? Some claim that these keys are still with us, but the truth is that they were never handed on to anyone. Peter took them with him to heaven when he died a martyr's death.

Note how Peter answered those who realised they had killed their promised Messiah and had asked the question: "'Brothers, what shall we do?" Peter replied, "Repent and be baptised every one of you, in the name of Jesus Christ for the forgiveness of your sins. And you will receive the gift of the Holy Spirit'" (Acts 2:37b,38).

Repentance is a vital step. To repent is to reform. 'It is not merely, Be sorry for what you have done wrong; nor is it, Resolve to do better; nor even, Try to amend your ways: but it is actual amendment of life from the views and the motives which the gospel of Christ exhibits' (Campbell).

To be baptised is to be immersed in water. There the sinner has his sins washed away. That's what Saul (later Paul) was told by Ananias (Acts 22:16). W. E. Vine in his *Expository Dictionary of New Testament Words* says: '*Baptisma*, baptism, consisting of the processes of immersion, submersion and emergence (from *bapto*, to dip) ...' Vine's words conform to the description of baptism by Paul in his Roman epistle. In it, he writes: 'We were therefore buried with Him through baptism into death in order that, just as Christ was raised from the dead through the glory of the Father, we too may live a new life' (6:4).

So what Paul is saying is that in baptism we identify ourselves with the death, burial and resurrection of the Lord. Jesus died. We must die. Jesus was buried. We must be buried. Jesus rose from the dead. We must rise from the dead to live a new life in Him. And let the right thing be done in the right way. To sprinkle, for example, is not to baptise. In fact, there is another Greek word for the verb 'to sprinkle' and it is *rhantizo*. This is *not* the word used by Paul in Romans.

Remember, Jesus began His ministry with baptism and ended it with baptism. He, of course, was immersed by John the Baptist or Baptizer (Matthew 3:13-17; Mark 1:9-11; Luke 3:21,22; John 1:29-34). And at the end the Lord said to His apostles: 'All authority in heaven and on earth has been given to me. Therefore go and make disciples of all nations, baptising them into the name of the Father and of the Son and of the Holy Spirit, and teaching them to obey everything I have commanded you. And surely I am with you always, to the very end of the age' (Matthew 28:18-20 – the last two verses of his record). Those who say that God cannot wash away sins in water would surely not deny that He once washed away Naaman's leprosy after he had dipped himself seven times in the Jordan river (2 Kings 5:14). If God did the latter then He can certainly do the former.

The steps of salvation are clear. One must repent in deed as well as word, and one must be baptised. Both are essential. We hear a lot today about the sinner's prayer. There are various forms of this prayer. For example, the following is often repeated: 'Dear Jesus, I am a sinner. I repent of my sins. Save me by your shed blood and come into my heart. I want to receive you as my personal Lord and Saviour. Amen'. No such prayer is found in the New Testament Scriptures. No one ever commanded such a prayer to be repeated by a sinner seeking salvation. What is commanded is repentance and baptism. This is important. Peter didn't need to tell them to believe because they already did believe. He didn't tell them to repeat the sinner's prayer. He most certainly did *not* say to them: 'You don't need to do anything because it has all been done for you'. No, what he did say was: 'Repent and be baptised every one of you ...' What was good enough for Peter on the day of Pentecost should be good enough for us now.

What is being said here in no way denigrates faith. To the Christian, faith is more than belief on Jesus. It is a trust and confidence in Him. Faith implies reliance upon God and obedience to God. The faith that saves is the faith that acts; the faith that is seen; the faith that takes steps; the faith that obeys; the faith that works through love, and that faith is never alone. James' words in his epistle on faith and deeds (2:14-26) are very telling and should be carefully considered.

It's one thing to get married and another thing to be a good husband or wife. It's one thing to have a child and another thing to be a good father or mother. It's one thing to become a child of God and another thing to grow in grace and in the knowledge of the Lord and remain His faithful servant unto death. The danger of falling away can be seen, for example, in the Master's Parable of the Sower

(Matthew 13:1-23; Mark 4:3-20; Luke 8:4-15). Truly, there are too many attractions and distractions in this world. In fact, the world itself can get in the way. One meaning of the word 'world' is: Pagan society with its false values and its false gods. John wrote:

Do not love the world or anything in the world. If anyone loves the world, the love of the Father is not in him. For everything in the world – the cravings of sinful man, the lust of his eyes and the boasting of what he has and does – comes not from the Father but from the world. The world and its desires pass away, but the man who does the will of God lives for ever (1 John 2:15-17).

We must be in the world, but not of it. The ship is fine on the ocean so long as the ocean is not in the ship. The ocean in the ship will sink it. The world in the saint will sink him. We have been warned!

# 8   Death – what then?

One day, the Lord will return, and everyone, the living and the dead, will be gathered on that day for judgment. We do not know when that day will come, but come it will. Yet we cannot help but wonder, what becomes of those of us who have died before that day? What does the Bible actually reveal about death?

Death is a separation, an alienation from life. Jesus Himself once tasted death and He tasted it for all. We know He died on a cross at a place called Calvary, the Place of the Skull. We read: 'And when Jesus cried out again in a loud voice, He gave up His spirit' (Matthew 27:50). Luke's record says: 'Jesus called out with a loud voice, "Father, into your hands I commend my spirit". When He had said this, He breathed His last' (23:46). John's gospel reads: 'When He had received the drink, Jesus said, "It is finished". With that He bowed His head and gave up His spirit' (19:30). But, earlier, Jesus had said to one of the repentant thieves crucified with Him: 'I tell you the truth, today you will be with me in paradise' (Luke

23:43). Paradise is a state within Hades to which all righteous souls are bound. The Jews knew paradise as Abraham's bosom. But there is also another state within Hades to which Jesus referred in His account of the rich man and Lazarus (Luke 16:19-31). It is a state in which the wicked experience torment (Luke 16:23). Note that the tables were turned for the rich man and Lazarus in the next world and there was, and still is, a fixed gulf between them.

They, like all the rest of the dead, await the coming judgment. Paul wrote: 'For we will all stand before God's judgment seat' (Romans 14:10b). Jesus Himself described the coming judgment in Matthew's gospel (25:31-46). Then there will be a formal separation of the righteous and the wicked, like the separation of sheep from goats. To those on His right He will say: 'Come you who are blessed by my Father; take your inheritance, the kingdom prepared for you since the creation of the world' (34). To those on His left (the vast majority) He will say: 'Depart from me, you who are cursed, into the eternal fire prepared for the devil and his angels' (41). Some of these are especially going to receive the shock of all shocks. For it was Jesus who once said in His famous Sermon on the Mount:

Not everyone who says to me, 'Lord, Lord' will enter the kingdom of heaven, but only he who does the will of my Father who is in heaven. Many will say to me on that day, 'Lord, Lord, did we not prophesy in your name, and in your name drive out demons and perform many miracles?' Then I will tell them plainly, 'I never knew you. Away from me, you evildoers!' (Matthew 7:21-23).

Jesus went on to say in that so-called sermon that it's not the sayers of His word that will be eternally saved, but the doers of His word (Matthew 7:24-27).

So the destination of every soul on earth is either heaven or hell. Heaven is the dwelling place of God. Heaven is eternal paradise. Heaven is eternal joy. Hell is the eternal state for the devil and his angels. It is also the eternal state for those who while on earth remained in the kingdom of darkness or the kingdom of Satan and who did not obey the gospel of Christ. Hell is eternal darkness. Hell is eternal torment. Make no mistake about it, heaven and hell are real. They are as real as America and Europe. They are real to Jesus and so they must be real to us.

The Book of Revelation, which uses a lot of symbolic language, nevertheless deals with the reality of both heaven and hell. For example we read:

Then I [John] saw a great white throne and Him who was seated on it. Earth and sky fled from His presence and there was no place for them. And I saw the dead, great and small, standing before the throne, and books were opened. Another book was opened, which is the book of life. The dead were judged according to what they had done as recorded in the books. The sea gave up the dead that were in it, and death and Hades gave up the dead that were in them, and each person was judged according to what he had done. Then death and Hades were thrown into the lake of fire. The lake of fire is the second death. If anyone's name was not found written in the book of life, he was thrown into the lake of fire (Revelation 20:11-15).

In the next chapter we have a description of the Holy City, the New Jerusalem. The terminology used is another way of describing heaven. We read:

And I [John] heard a loud voice from the throne saying, 'Now the dwelling of God is with men, and He will live with them. They will be His people, and God Himself will be with them and be their God. He will wipe away every tear from their eyes. There will be no more death or mourning or crying or pain, for the old order of things has passed away' (21:3,4).

At the beginning of the chapter John also wrote: 'Then I saw a new heaven and a new earth, for the first heaven and the first earth had passed away, and there was no longer any sea' (21:1). So it's all change – sun, moon and stars gone and earth itself gone. Peter has written:

But the day of the Lord [the last day] will come like a thief. The heavens will disappear with a roar; the elements will be destroyed by fire, and the earth and everything in it will be burned up. Since everything will be destroyed in this way, what kind of people ought you to be? You ought to live holy and godly lives as you look forward eagerly to the day of God and speed its coming. That day will bring about the destruction of the heavens by fire, and the elements will melt in the heat. But in keeping with His promise we are looking forward to a new heaven and a new earth, the home of righteousness (2 Peter 3:10-13).

Surely heaven is worth striving for and hell worth avoiding at all costs!

There is hope! It's not all doom and gloom. Other New Testament passages on the theme of hope are worth considering.

Blessed are you when people insult you, persecute you and falsely say all kinds of evil against you because of me [Jesus]. Rejoice and be glad, because great is your reward in heaven, for in the same way they persecuted the prophets who were before you (Matthew 5:11,12).

I [Paul] consider that our present sufferings are not worth comparing with the glory that will be revealed in us (Romans 8:18).

This grace was given us in Christ Jesus before the beginning of time, but it has now been revealed through the appearing of our Saviour, Christ Jesus, who has destroyed death and has brought life and immortality to light through the gospel (2 Timothy 1:9b,10).

For the grace of God that brings salvation has appeared to all men. It teaches us to say 'No' to ungodliness and worldly passions, and to live self-controlled, upright and godly lives in this present age, while we wait for the blessed hope – the glorious appearing of our great God and Saviour, Jesus Christ, who gave Himself for us to redeem us from all wickedness and to purify for Himself a people that are His very own, eager to do what is good (Titus 2:11-14).

Praise be to the God and Father of our Lord Jesus Christ! In His great mercy He has given us new birth into a living hope through the resurrection of Jesus Christ from the dead (1 Peter 1:3).

Anyone who studies from the Scriptures the Jewish system and the Christian system will readily see that they are not the same. The former looked exclusively to this present world; the latter, primarily, and almost exclusively, looks to the next.

The eternal keeps everything in perspective. As has been said: 'Time is given us to enable us to prepare for eternity; to train and discipline our spirits for the high and noble destiny which God would have us to enjoy, in His presence, for ever'. Or to put it another way: 'All time is, indeed, but the preface of the great volumes of man's glorious and eternal destiny'.

Time is short. Life on earth is brief. What is written in James warns us never to take this life for granted:

> Now listen, you who say, 'Today or tomorrow we will go to this or that city, spend a year there, carry on business and make money'. Why, you do not even know what will happen tomorrow. What is your life? You are a mist that appears for a little while and then vanishes. Instead, you ought to say, 'If it is the Lord's will, we will live and do this or that' (James 4:13-15).

# 9  And so ... have FAITH!

Christianity is either true or false. The writer of this book, after studying it, preaching it, teaching it and writing about it and, indeed, trying to live it for nearly fifty years, believes with all his heart that it is true.

He sees it as differing from all other major religious systems of the world in that it is essentially historical. Other religious systems are based upon human philosophy, speculation or mysticism.

Christianity primarily and exclusively looks to the next world. But Christianity is not like a life insurance policy from which one only benefits by dying. There are also tremendous dividends in this life. And there is much truth in the statement: 'There is a great deal more to Christianity than keeping people out of hell. It also involves keeping hell out of people'.

In 1829, Alexander Campbell and Robert Owen, the famous socialist reformer best known for putting his principles into practice at New Lanark in Scotland, met in debate in America. The debate was published in a book entitled: *Debate on the Evidences of Christianity*. Campbell wrote in the introduction:

> Christianity is a positive institution and has had a positive existence in the world for more than eighteen centuries. Infidelity [unbelief], as opposed to Christianity, is not an institution, but a mere negation of an institution and of the facts and documents upon which it is founded ... The unbeliever is but the incarnation of a negative idea. He is absolutely but a mere negation. He stands to Christianity as darkness stands to light. Is darkness anything? Is blindness anything but the loss of sight? Is unbelief anything but the repudiation of evidence? ... To my mind, it has long been a moral demonstration, clear as the sun, that no one could have drawn a character, such as that of Jesus Christ, from all the stores of human learning, from all the resources of the human imagination. The simple character of Jesus Christ weighs more in the eyes of cultivated reason than all the miracles he ever wrought. No greater truth was ever uttered with these words: 'He that has seen me has seen the Father also.'

Belief in Jesus is more than a matter of life and death – it is a matter of life *over* death. The biggest question anyone can answer is: 'What do you think of Christ?' And there can be no neutrality about Him. He once said: 'He who is not with me is against me and he who does not gather with me scatters' (Matthew 12:30). One day we shall all have to face Him.

On the last day we shall all be judged by what He has said. Hearken to His words!

As for the person who hears my words but does not keep them, I do not judge him. For I did not come to judge the world, but to save it. There is a judge for the one who rejects me and does not accept my words; that very word which I spoke will condemn him at the last day. For I did not speak of my own accord, but the Father who sent me commanded me what to say and how to say it. I know that His command leads to eternal life. So whatever I say is just what the Father has told me to say (John 12:47-50).

So we see how vitally important it is when it comes to Christ to … have FAITH! in Him.

# Further reading

Alexander, Pat *The Lion Handbook to the Bible*, 4th edn, Oxford, Lion Hudson, 2009

Andrews, Edgar *Who made God?* Darlington, EP Books, 2009

Barclay, William *Flesh and Spirit*, Edinburgh, The Saint Andrew Press, 2012

Barclay, William *The Daily Study Bible*, rev. edn 17 vols., Edinburgh, The Saint Andrew Press, 1975. (Note individual volumes are available separately.)

Berlinski, David *The Devil's Delusion*, New York, Basic Books, 2009

Blanchard, John *Does God Believe in Atheists?* Darlington, EP Books, 2000

Blanchard, John *Whatever Happened to Hell?* Darlington, EP Books, 2004

Bruce, F. F. *Jesus: Past, Present and Future*, Westmont IL, InterVarsity Press, 1998

Bruce, F. F. *History of the Bible in English*, 3rd ed. London, Oxford University Press, 1978

Bruce, F. F. *Jesus & Christian Origins Outside the New Testament*, Grand Rapids, MI, Eerdmans Publishing

Co., 1974

Bruce, F. F. *The Books and the Parchments*, Grand Rapids MI, Fleming H Revell Co., 1984

Budgeon, Victor *The Charismatics and the Word of God*, Darlington, Evangelical Press, 2001

Burgess, Stuart *He Made the Stars Also*, Leominster, DayOne Publications, 2012

Burgess, Stuart *The Origin of Man*, Leominster, DayOne Publications, 2005

Campbell, Alexander *The Christian System*, London, Forgotten Books, 2012

Craig, William Lane *On Guard: Defending Your Faith with Reason and Precision*, Colorado Springs CO, David C Cook, 2010

Devlin, Patrick *The Enforcement of Morals*, London, Oxford University Press, 1965

DeYoung, Donald B. *Astronomy and the Bible*, Winona IN, BMH Books, 2010

Ferrie, Dr Alastair *Evangelism in a Post Christian Culture*, Bloomington IN, iUniverse, 2008

Fisher, Graham *Why Believe in Adam?* Aylesbury, Eye-Opener Publications, 1989

Flew, Anthony *There is a God*, New York, HarperOne, 2007

Gascoigne, Bamber *The Christians*, London, Jonathan Cape, 1977

Geisler, Norman L. and Frank Turek *I Don't Have Enough Faith to Be an Atheist*, Wheaton IL, Crossway Books, 2004

Geisler, Norman L. and William E. Nix *A General Introduction to the Bible*, 2nd edn, Chicago IL, Moody Publishers, 1995

Geisler, Norman L. *If God, Why Evil?* Bloomington MN, Bethany House Publishers, 2011

Green, Michael *I Believe in the Holy Spirit*, Grand Rapids, MI, William B. Eerdmans Publishing Company, 2004

Hurt, John M. *Bible Correspondence Course*, Smyrna TN, Hurt Publications (available from the author of this book)

Johnson, Phillip E. *Testing Darwinism*, Nottingham, Inter-Varsity Press, 1997

Jones, Simon *The World of the Early Church*, Oxford, Lion Hudson, 2011

Ketcherside, W. Carl *Heaven Help Us (The Holy Spirit in Your Life)*, Kindle edition, SCM e-prints, 2010

Ketcherside, W. Carl *Simple Trusting Faith*, Kindle Edition, SCM e-prints, 2011

Kitchen, K. A. *On the Reliability of the Old Testament*, Grand Rapids, MI, William B Eerdmans Publishing Co, 2006

Kitchen, K. A. *The Bible in its World*, Eugene OR,

Wipf & Stock Publishers, 2004

Lennox, John C. *God's Undertaker: Has Science Buried God?* Oxford, Lion Books, 2009

Lewis, C. S. *Mere Christianity*, London, William Collins 2012

Lewis, C. S. *The Problem of Pain*, London, William Collins, 2012

Marshall, I. Howard *I Believe in the Historical Jesus*, Vancouver, Regent College Publishing, 2001

Marshall, I. Howard *The Work of Christ*, Grand Rapids, MI, Zondervan, 1970

Marshall, I. Howard, A. R. Millard, J. I. Packer and Donald J. Wiseman *New Bible Dictionary*, Nottingham, Inter-Varsity Press, 1996

Martin, James *Suffering Man, Loving God*, Glasgow, Fount Paperbacks, 1979

McDowell, Josh *Evidence That Demands a Verdict*, rev. edn, Milton Keynes, Authentic Lifestyle, 1999

McGrath, Alister *The Unknown God*, Grand Rapids, MI, William B Eerdmans Publishing Co, 1999

Millard, Alan *Discoveries from the Time of Jesus*, Oxford, Lion Books, 1993

Millard, Alan *Treasures from Bible Times*, Oxford, Lion Books, 1985

Morris, Henry M. *Science and the Bible*, Chicago IL, Moody Publishers, 1986

Oliver, Lancelot *New Testament Christianity*, Birmingham, Publishing Committee of Churches of Christ, 1911

Pawson, David *Unlocking the Bible Omnibus*, London, Collins, 2007

Pearcey, Nancy *Total Truth*, Wheaton IL, Crossway Books, 2008

Schaeffer, Francis A. *How Should We Then Live?* Wheaton IL, Crossway Books, 2005

Sinclair, Alistair J. *What Is Philosophy? An Introduction*, Edinburgh, Dunedin, 2008

Smith, F. LaGard *Baptism – the Believer's Wedding Ceremony*, Nashville TN, Gospel Advocate Company, 1993

Stark, Rodney *The Triumph of Christianity*, New York, HarperOne, 2011

Stott, John R. W. *Christ the Controversialist*, London, Inter-Varsity Press, 1970

Stott, John R. W. *Understanding the Bible,* rev. edn, Grand Rapids MI, Zondervan, 2003

Strobel, Lee *The Case for a Creator*, Grand Rapids MI, Zondervan, 2005

Thompson, J. A. *Handbook of Life in Bible Times*, Nottingham, Inter-Varsity Press, 1987

Veith, Gene Edward *Guide to Contemporary Culture*, Leicester, Crossway Books, 1994

Water, Mark *Encyclopedia of Bible Facts*, Alresford, John Hunt Publishing, 2003

Wenham, Gordon J., J. Alec Motyer, Donald A. Carson and R. T. France *New Bible Commentary*, Nottingham, Inter-Varsity Press, 1994

White, Dr A. J. Monty *Wonderfully Made*, Darlington, Evangelical Press, 1989

Wilder-Smith, A. E. *Man's Origin, Man's Destiny*, Bloomington MN, Bethany House, 1975

Williams, Peter S. *A Sceptic's Guide to Atheism*, Milton Keynes, Paternoster Press, 2009

Yamauchi, Edwin *The World of the First Christians*, 2nd edn, Oxford, Lion Books, 1982

Young, E. J. *An Introduction to the Old Testament*, rev. edn, Grand Rapids, MI, William B. Eerdmans Publishing Company, 1984

A useful magazine, published quarterly:
*The Scripture Standard*
Email: AshurstA@aol.com
And a valuable website:
www.TeachMeThyWay.org.uk

The above listing is far from exhaustive. The author is pleased to provide details on request of other helpful books relevant to the chapter headings. But keep in mind that these books contain the words of men. There is one Book above them all: and the words of men must always be judged by the Word of God.